SCIENCE
NEWS
for
KIDS

Space and Astronomy

SCIENCE
NEWS for
KIDS

SCIENCE
NEWS for
KIDS

Space and Astronomy

Series Editor
Tara Koellhoffer

With a Foreword by
Emily Sohn,
Science News for Kids

CHELSEA
CLUBHOUSE
An Imprint of Chelsea House Publishers

Space and Astronomy

J 520 Koelhoffer

Copyright © 2006 by Infobase Publishing

Chelsea Clubhouse
An imprint of Chelsea House Publishers
132 West 31st Street
New York NY 10001

For Library of Congress Cataloging-in-Publication Data, please contact the publisher.

ISBN 0-7910-9125-2

You can find Chelsea House on the World Wide Web at
http://www.chelseahouse.com

Text and cover design by Takeshi Takahashi
Layout by Ladybug Editorial & Design

Printed in the United States of America

Bang   10 9 8 7 6 5 4 3 2 1

This book is printed on acid-free paper.

All links, web addresses, and Internet search terms were checked and verified to be correct at the time of publication. Because of the dynamic nature of the web, some addresses and links may have changed since publication and may no longer be valid.

Contents Overview

Detailed Table of Contents

Detailed Table of Contents

by Emily Sohn
Science News for Kids

Science, for many kids, is just another subject in school. You may have biology tests and astronomy quizzes to study for, chemistry formulas to memorize, physics problems to work through, or current events to report on. All of it, after a while, can seem like a major drag.

Now, forget about all that, and think about your day. What did you eat for breakfast? How did you get to school and what did you think about along the way? What makes the room bright enough for you to see this book? How does the room stay cool or warm enough for you to be comfortable? What do you like to do for fun?

All of your answers, in some way, involve science. Food, transportation, electricity, toys, video games, animals, plants, your brain, the rest of your body: Behind the scenes of nearly anything you can think of, there are scientists trying to figure out how it works, how it came to be, or how to make it better. Science can explain why pizza and chocolate taste good. Science gives airplanes a lift. And science is behind the medicines that make your aches and pains go away. Most exciting of all, science never stands still.

Science News for Kids tracks the trends and delves into the discoveries that make life more interesting and more efficient every day. The stories in these volumes explore a tiny fraction of the grand scope of research happening around the world. These stories point out the questions that push scientists to probe ever deeper into physics, chemistry, biology, psychology, and more. Reading about the challenges of science will spark in you the same sort of curiosity that drives researchers to keep searching for answers, despite setbacks and failed experiments. The stories here may even inspire you to seek out your own solutions to the world's puzzles.

Being a scientist is hard work, but it can be one of the best jobs around. You may picture scientists always tinkering away in their labs, pouring chemicals into flasks and reading technical papers. Well, they do those things some of the time. But they also get to dig around in the dirt, blow things up, and even ride rockets into outer space. They travel around the world. They save lives. And, they get to spend most of their time thinking about the things that fascinate them most, all in the name of work.

Sometimes, researchers have revelations that change the way we think about the universe. Albert Einstein, for one, explained light, space, time, and other aspects of the physical world in radically new terms. He's perhaps the most famous scientist in history, thanks to his theories of relativity and other ideas. Likewise, James Watson and

Francis Crick forever changed the face of medicine when they first described the structure of the genetic material DNA in 1953. Today, doctors use information about DNA to explain why some people are likely to develop certain diseases and why others may have trouble reading or doing math. Police investigators rely on DNA to solve mysteries when they analyze hairs, blood, saliva, and remains at the scene of a crime. And scientists are now eagerly pursuing potential uses of DNA to cure cancer and other diseases.

Science can be about persistence and courage as much as it is about grand ideas. Society doesn't always welcome new ideas. Before Galileo Galilei became one of the first people to point a telescope at the sky in the early 1600s, for example, nearly everyone believed that the planets revolved around Earth. Galileo discovered four moons orbiting Jupiter. He saw that Venus has phases, like the moon. And he noticed spots on the sun and lumps on the moon's craggy face. All of these observations shook up the widely held view that the heavens were perfect, orderly, and centered on Earth. Galileo's ideas were so controversial, in fact, that he was forced to deny them to save his life. Even then, he was sentenced to imprisonment in his own home.

Since Galileo's time, the public has so completely accepted his views of the universe that space missions have been named after him, as have craters on the moon and on Mars. In 1969, Neil Armstrong became the first person to stand on the moon. Now, astronauts spend months in orbit, living on an international space station, floating in weightlessness. Spacecraft have landed on planets and moons as far away as Saturn. One probe recently slammed into a comet to collect information. With powerful telescopes, astronomers continue to spot undiscovered moons in our solar system, planets orbiting stars in other parts of our galaxy, and evidence of the strange behavior of black holes. New technologies continue to push the limits of what we can detect in outer space and what we know about how the universe formed.

Here on Earth, computer technology has transformed society in a short period of time. The first electronic digital computers, which appeared in the 1940s, took up entire rooms and weighed thousands of pounds. Decades passed before people started using their own PCs (personal computers) at home. Laptops came even later.

These days, it's hard to imagine life without computers. They track restaurant orders. They help stores process credit cards. They allow you to play video games, send e-mails and instant messages to your friends, and write reports that you can edit and print without ever picking up a pen. Doctors use computers to diagnose their patients, and banks use computers to keep track of our money. As computers become more and more popular, they continue to get smaller, more powerful, less expensive, and more integrated into our lives in ways we don't even notice.

Probes that fly to Pluto and computers the size of peas are major advances that don't happen overnight. Science is a process of small steps, and a new discovery often starts with a single question. Why, for example, do hurricanes and tsunamis form? What is it like at the center of Earth? Why do some types of french fries taste better than others? Research projects can also begin with observations. There are fewer tigers in India than there used to be, for instance. Kids now weigh more than they did a generation ago. Mars shows signs that the planet once supported life.

The next step is investigation, which can take on many forms, depending on the subject. Brain researchers, for one, often do experiments in their laboratories with the help of sophisticated equipment. In one type of neuroscience study, subjects repeatedly solve tasks while machines measure activity in their brains. Some environmental scientists who study climate, on the other hand, collect data by tracking weather patterns over the years. Paleontologists dig deep into the earth to look for clues about what the world was like when dinosaurs were alive. Anthropologists learn about other cultures by talking to people and collecting stories. Doctors monitor large numbers of patients taking a new drug or no drug to figure out whether a drug is safe and effective before others can use it.

Designing studies requires creativity, and scientists spend many years training to use the tools of their profession. Physicists need to learn complicated mathematical formulas. Ecologists make models that simulate interactions between species. Physicians learn the name of every bone and blood vessel in the body. The most basic tools, however, are ones that everyone has: our senses. The best way to start learning about the world through science is to pay attention to what you smell, taste, see, hear, and feel. Notice. Ask questions. Collect data. Do experiments. Draw tentative conclusions. Ask more questions.

Most importantly, leave no stone unturned. There's no limit to the topics available for research. Robots, computers, and new technologies in medicine are the waves of the future. Just as important, however, are studies of the past. Figuring out what Earth's climate used to be like and which animals and plants used to live here are the first steps toward understanding how the planet is changing and what those changes might mean for our future. And don't forget to look around at what's going on around you, right now. You might just be surprised at how many subjects you can find to investigate.

Ready to get started? The stories in this book are great sources of inspiration. Each of the articles comes directly from the *Science News for Kids* Website, which you can find online at *http://sciencenewsforkids.org*. All articles at the site, which is updated weekly, cover current events in science, and all are written with middle-school students in mind. If anything you read in this book sparks your interest, feel free to visit the Website to check out the latest developments and find out more.

And keep an eye out for an occasional feature called "News Detective." These essays describe what it's like to be a science journalist, roaming the world in search of scientists at work. Science writing is an often-overlooked career possibility, but science writers have endless opportunities to learn about many things at once, to share in the excitement of scientific discovery, and to help scientists get the word out about the significance of their work.

So, go ahead and turn the page. There's so much left to discover.

Section 1

Stars

When you look up at the night sky, what do you see? Maybe you see all the twinkling lights of the distant stars and think about the vastness and mystery of the universe. Maybe you squint your eyes and try to pick out the constellations you learned about in school or at the planetarium. Or maybe you ponder the notion that because each of those seemingly tiny stars is actually a sun very much like ours, it's possible there could be other planets—and other living beings— somewhere out there in the universe. In this section, we look at different kinds of stars and the roles they play in forming the stuff of the universe.

In the first article, author Emily Sohn examines astronomers' findings that objects in space—including stars—have limits on how big they can get. The second article talks about massive clusters made up of many stars. For a long time, scientists thought these huge star clusters only existed in faraway galaxies, but new discoveries have shown that one of them can be found right here in our own Milky Way galaxy.

Stars are more than far-off suns—they serve many useful purposes for scientists studying the origin of the universe. In the third article, author Emily Sohn explains how astronomers use stars to pinpoint how old the universe is.

Finally, we learn about how stars are born. Emily Sohn takes us deep into outer space to show how the process of creating new stars works.

—The Editor

A Limit to Star Size

Recent findings have shown that, like almost everything
else in the universe, stars are limited in how big they can
get. Just as people can only grow so tall, stars can only
reach a certain size—and scientists believe they have figured out what size that is. As author Emily Sohn explains
in this article, astronomers studying a group of young
stars called the Arches cluster have determined the
upper limit of star size.

—The Editor

No Fat Stars

by Emily Sohn

There's a limit to how big most things can get. Some people are really tall, but no one is as tall as a house. Cats can get really fat, but there's never been a tabby as heavy as a truck. And so on.

Now, astronomer Don Figer of the Space Telescope Science Institute in Baltimore has discovered that the size of a star may have a limit, too. No stars in our **galaxy**, he estimates, can weigh more than 150 times the mass of our sun.

This conclusion comes from observations of an area near the center of the Milky Way called the Arches cluster. The cluster is between 2 million and 2.5 million years old, and stars are still forming there. It contains about 2,000 stars.

Figer thought that the Arches cluster would be a good place to search for the galaxy's biggest stars because it's still fairly young (Figure 1.1). Massive stars have short lives, so it wouldn't make sense to look at a cluster that was much older than Arches. It also wouldn't make sense to look at much younger ones because stars in young clusters are still hidden behind gas and dust.

The Arches cluster was also promising because it's

big. Its total mass is that of about 10,000 suns. In theory, it could hold at least 18 stars weighing more than 130 times the mass of the sun.

Using the Hubble Space Telescope to gauge the weight of hundreds of stars in the Arches cluster, Figer found no stars this big. This means, he concluded, that there must be an upper limit to the size of a star—perhaps about 150 times the sun's mass.

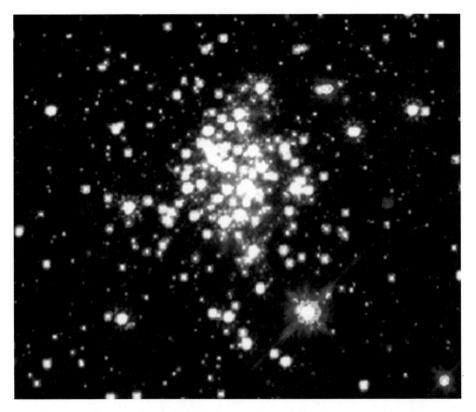

Figure 1.1 The Arches cluster is a group of young stars in the center of the Milky Way galaxy.

Three Star Systems

Original Calculations for the Habitable Zone in Trinary Star Systems
Alistair Thompson Hayden, 14, Ann Arbor, Michigan
Intel Achievement Award, Intel International Science and
Engineering Fair, 2004

Many stars in our galaxy are members of multiple-star systems. In searching for extraterrestrial life, it is important for us to know which star systems are habitable. The purpose of this project was to establish whether planets in trinary star systems can be habitable. To determine this, Alistair used the laws of physics to write a computer program to simulate the orbits of the three stars in hierarchical trinary systems (binary systems in which one component is itself binary) and one planet orbiting the solitary component. Then Alistair found whether the planet was capable of supporting life for long periods of time based on the total amount of energy received from all three stars.

In this project, Alistair showed that habitable planets can indeed exist in trinary star systems, though not in all instances. In addition, he found that, as the third component was moved further away from the binary component, the time period of the "envelope" containing the energy fluctuations as well as the stability of the entire system increased.

Astronomers are just beginning to understand the processes behind star birth. No one yet knows what determines the limits on their growth. Figer plans to study clusters of different ages to find out more.

Going Deeper:

Cowen, Ron. "Weighing in on a Star: A Stellar Size Limit." *Science News* 167 (March 12, 2005): 164–165. Available online at *http:// www.sciencenews.org/articles/20050312/ fob4.asp*.

Stars Help Show How Old the Universe Is

You probably learned in science class that the universe is billions upon billions of years old. But did you ever wonder how scientists know this? One way astronomers can date the origins of the universe is by looking at stars. A star radiates huge amounts of heat and light, and a star's brightness and strength can tell astronomers a lot about its age. The older the stars, the older the universe, as writer Emily Sohn explains in the following article.

—The Editor

Older Stars, New Age for the Universe

by Emily Sohn

The universe has been around for an extra long time.

Astronomers used to estimate that the oldest stars were about 13 billion years old. New data suggest that these stars are nearly a billion years older than that.

For most of its life, a star produces energy and heat by fusing hydrogen to make helium inside its core. Near the end of its life, when its hydrogen supply is running low, the star continues to convert hydrogen into helium but requires the presence of carbon, nitrogen, and oxygen to do so.

Two teams of scientists have now used **particle accelerators**—atom smashers—to mimic the conditions inside stars. By studying high-energy collisions between hydrogen nuclei (**protons**) and nitrogen nuclei, the researchers could check how quickly nuclear reactions inside a star proceed.

Both groups, one at the University of North Carolina at Chapel Hill and the other at the National Institute for Nuclear Physics in Italy, found that the reactions occur only half as fast as had been estimated.

Such a slow reaction time allows **gravity** to shrink a

star more than it would if the reaction were faster. As a result, an elderly star looks brighter than it otherwise would. Brightness is supposed to indicate how old a star is.

Now that they know how deceptive brightness can be, astronomers have had to revise their estimates of star age.

In line with observations from a **satellite** called the Wilkinson Microwave Anisotropy Probe, the universe now appears to be about 13.7 billion years old, astronomers say. That's quite a lot of time to ponder.

Going Deeper:

Cowen, Ron. "Old Stars Even Older: Determining a New Age for the Universe." *Science News* 165 (May 22, 2004): 323. Available online at *http://www.sciencenews.org/articles/20040522/fob1.asp*.

Birth of a Star

Like everything else, stars have to be "born"—and this birth can be a long and difficult process. Astronomers weren't always sure how stars were formed, but thanks to a recently discovered object that is taking on a faint star-like glow, they believe they are witnessing a star being born. In the next article, Emily Sohn examines the early life of a new star.

—The Editor

Baby Star

by Emily Sohn

In Hollywood, a hit movie can make an actor a big star overnight. In outer space, star birth takes a bit longer.

Astronomers have now observed what they suggest is a baby star in the process of being born (Figure 1.2). If they're right, it'll be the earliest twinkles ever picked up from a newborn star.

Through a telescope in outer space, the object looks like a faintly glowing body. Astronomers from the

Figure 1.2 This NASA photograph shows a young star soon after its "birth."

University of Texas in Austin spotted it with the Spitzer Space Telescope, which orbits Earth.

The object lies 6,000 light years from Earth in a thick cloud of gas and dust called L1014. In the past, L1014 has appeared totally dark. When the Spitzer team recently pointed the telescope at the cloud's center, though, they were surprised to see a spot of infrared light that looked like "a big, red, bloodshot eye." Infrared light isn't visible to the human eye, but all objects absorb and give off this form of radiation.

At such an early stage in its life, the object has a tiny mass. Compared to our sun, it weighs in at less than one thousandth the sun's mass.

No one is sure what will happen next. One possibility is that the glimmering body will gather together enough gas and dust to become a true star. It's also possible that the object will run out of steam and instead turn into a faint, cold object known as a **brown dwarf**.

In the star nursery, only time will tell.

Going Deeper:

Cowen, Ron. "First Light: Faint Object May Be Youngest Star Detected." *Science News* 166 (November 13, 2004): 309. Available online at *http://www.sciencenews.org/articles/20041113/fob5.asp*.

Section 2

Galaxies

You've probably heard of galaxies and may even know that our planet is part of the Milky Way galaxy (opposite). But would you be able to explain precisely what a galaxy is? In the March 2003 issue of *Natural History*, author Charles Liu makes an interesting description: "Galaxies in the universe are rather like the cells in an animal. Just as cells combine to make an animal's organs and systems, so, too, do galaxies come together to make the superclusters . . . that define the large-scale structure of the cosmos. Not surprisingly, in much the same way that biologists examine cell development to understand the aging process in animals, astronomers study galaxy formation to decipher the **evolution** of the cosmos."

There are three main types of galaxies: spiral, elliptical, and irregular. All of them are systems of stars, gases, dust, and dark matter bound together by gravity. Our own Milky Way galaxy is a spiral galaxy 100,000 light years in diameter, and it is not the largest one. Some galaxies are several hundred thousand light years in diameter. In this section, we take a look at the most fascinating features of some of the galaxies of the universe.

—The Editor

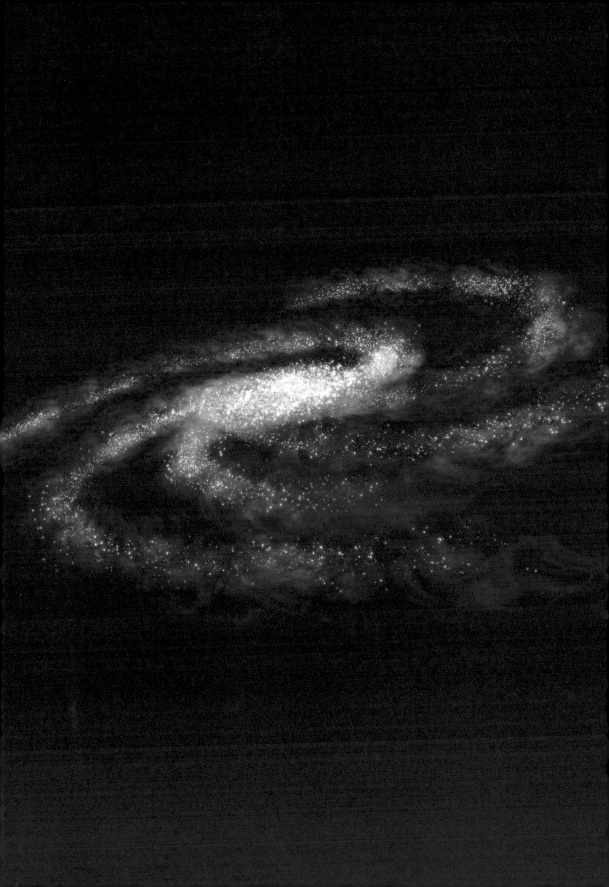

When Galaxies Collide

Anything that moves might eventually crash into something else. This holds true even for galaxies—the massive
collections of stars and other celestial bodies that make
up the substance of our universe. In the following article,
writer Emily Sohn looks at the phenomenon of crashing
galaxies, and what these outer space "accidents" mean
for the future of the universe.

—The Editor

Clash of the Galaxies

by Emily Sohn

Being in a car accident or train wreck would be scary enough. But can you imagine getting caught in a galaxy wreck?

A new image might give you an idea of what that would be like. Astronomers have taken a picture of an enormous collision between two of the universe's most massive clusters of galaxies. The merging clusters each contain hundreds of galaxies and millions upon millions of stars. It's the most powerful cosmic collision yet recorded in such a clear image.

There are just a few hundred large galaxy clusters in the universe, scientists estimate. Between 20 and 30 of them are probably crashing into each other and merging right now (Figure 2.1).

To get the new image, astronomers from the University of Honolulu in Hawaii used the European Space Agency's orbiting XMM-Newton telescope. They pointed it at a cluster called Abell 754, which is 800 million light years away from Earth. The cluster contains about 1,000 galaxies.

The astronomers already knew that Abell 754 was in the middle of some kind of collision, but they weren't

Figure 2.1 This photograph shows the crashing collision of two galaxies, seen as the glowing merged object at center.

sure of all the details. By detecting X-rays produced by the cluster, they were able to pick out huge shock waves hurled into outer space by the collision.

The X-ray patterns revealed that the second cluster involved in the collision was smaller than Abell 754 and contained about 300 galaxies. Further analysis also indicated that the smaller cluster had plowed into the bigger one.

The collision has been going on for about 300 million years, and it's not over yet. After a few billion years more, the two clusters will be fully merged into one.

Now that's no small fender bender!

Going Deeper:

Cowen, Ron. "Big Smash: Galaxy Clusters in Collision." *Science News* 166 (October 2, 2004): 211–212. Available online at *http://www.sciencenews.org/articles/20041002/fob2.asp*.

A Dark Mystery

As we discussed earlier, galaxies are made up of stars and other celestial bodies—very often, things that give off or reflect light, things that can be seen. But there may be another type of galaxy that is very different from the star-packed kind we're used to. Scientists have recently discovered strange clusters of dark space that seem to be galaxies—but they are galaxies without the light of stars. In the next article, author Emily Sohn explores this baffling mystery.

—The Editor

Dark Galaxy

by Emily Sohn

The Milky Way is packed with stars, comets, asteroids, moons, and planets, including our own. Other galaxies in the universe are similarly crammed full of stars and various objects.

Astronomers have now spied something very unusual. They've found a patch of space that looks empty but actually appears to be a galaxy that contains no stars. Theorists had proposed that such "dark" galaxies could exist, but no one had ever seen one before.

The mysterious object is in an area of space known as the Virgo cluster of galaxies. This cluster is the closet one to the Milky Way and contains more than 100 galaxies of various types, including spiral and elliptical galaxies. In 2000, astronomers at Cardiff University in Wales noticed that this vast region has a pair of isolated clouds made up of hydrogen gas.

Further observations revealed that one of the clouds is associated with a faintly glowing galaxy. This makes sense because balls of hydrogen gas usually indicate an area where stars are forming.

The other hydrogen ball, however, appears to have no glowing galaxy as a partner. Yet, other observations suggest that it's part of a massive object weighing as much as a galaxy of 100 billion suns.

The astronomers propose that the object, named VIRGOHI21, is full of a mysterious substance called dark matter. And they say there might be many more galaxies just like it. Astronomers just haven't spotted them yet.

For now, there's a lot of explaining to do.

"Seeing a dark galaxy—a galaxy without any stars— is like seeing a city without any people," says astronomer Robert Minchin of Cardiff University. "We want to know why nobody lives there."

Going Deeper:

Shiga, David. "Ghostly Galaxy: Massive, Dark Cloud Intrigues Scientists." *Science News* **167 (February 26, 2005): 131. Available online at** *http://www.sciencenews.org/articles/20050226/ fob1.asp*.

Colorful Galaxies

Most of see the stars in the sky and assume that they are all just like they look: yellowish-white in color. In fact, stars—and the galaxies they form—come in a wide variety of colors, from white to red to blue. This may not seem very surprising, but here's something that is: As author Emily Sohn explains in the following article, galaxies of different colors prefer to stay close to others of the same hue.

—The Editor

Galaxies Divide Sharply Along Color Lines

by Emily Sohn

When most people look at the night sky, they see lots of twinkling white spots. In fact, stars come in a variety of colors, from red to blue. And like soccer teams at a tournament, galaxies seem to organize themselves by hue.

Astronomers now report that old, red galaxies clump together much more tightly than do young, blue ones. And there doesn't seem to be any middle ground.

The astronomers, from Johns Hopkins University in Baltimore, used data from the Sloan Digital Sky Survey. It's the largest survey of galaxies ever done, with about 50 million galaxies already viewed. The Sloan survey, which uses a telescope in New Mexico, is also unique because it sorts galaxies by color.

Old galaxies look red because old, cooler stars give off mostly red light. Young galaxies are full of hot stars that formed more recently and still give off bluish light.

After analyzing 2 million galaxies, the researchers noticed two distinct types of galaxy clumping: very tight or very loose, based on age and color.

The new finding about galaxy distribution and color

might help explain some things about what happens to galaxies as they get older. It might also provide hints about dark matter—mysterious stuff that may fill the universe, according to some astronomers, even though no one has ever seen it.

Going Deeper:

Cowen, Ron. "Red Team, Blue Team: Galaxy Survey Shows That Color Matters." *Science News* 163 (May 31, 2003): 341. Available online at *http://www.sciencenews.org/20030531/fob6.asp*.

Section 3

Planets and Moons

If you're like most people, you learned in school that there are nine planets in our solar system: Earth, Mars, Neptune, Venus, Saturn, Uranus, Jupiter, Mercury, and Pluto. You might be surprised to learn that scientists have been fiercely debating this seemingly obvious fact. Astronomers have long defined a *planet* a large celestial object that orbits around a star (as our planets orbit around the Sun), but there is widespread disagreement over how to refine that definition. How big must an object be to be considered a planet? Some scientists believe that Pluto is too small to be a true planet. If we followed their logic, we would have only eight planets in our solar system. On the other hand, some people argue that certain smaller objects deserve to be included in the list of our solar system's planets. According to this argument, we might have to recognize dozens of celestial bodies as planets.

If identifying the members of our own solar system isn't difficult enough, there's also the matter of discovering planets *outside* our solar system. What standards should be used in those cases? How do we determine whether an object we can't actually see is a planet or not? How do we tell the difference between a small planet and a large moon? In this section, we look at the fascinating science of finding, naming, and learning about planets and the moons that revolve around them.

—The Editor

Finding New Planets

Scientists have known for many years that there are other planets out there, beyond our solar system, orbiting around other suns. That's not necessarily big news, since astronomers have been searching for these planets for a long time. What's most interesting is that some of the newfound planets seem to resemble Earth in size and composition. If other Earth-like planets do exist, then the possibility that life could exist on other planets becomes ever more likely. In the following two articles, author Emily Sohn examines some of the latest findings in the search for previously unknown planets.

—The Editor

Planet Hunters Nab Three More

by Emily Sohn

There are other planets around other stars in other solar systems. That's the old news.

Now, new observations have turned up the three smallest, most Earth-like planets ever found outside our **solar system**. Each one weighs between 14 and 25 times the mass of Earth. That makes them about the size of Neptune.

Until now, none of the **extrasolar** planets discovered so far has looked anything like Earth. Out of about 135 such planets, nearly all are roughly 300 times Earth's mass. That's the same size as Jupiter, the biggest planet in the solar system. And like Jupiter, they're all big balls of gas around a solid core of rock and ice. Smaller, rocky planets like Earth are much harder to detect.

With advances in technology, however, the view is getting better. The new planets are so small and far away that astronomers still can't see them directly. Instead, they look for tiny wobbles in the motion of a planet's star, caused by the planet's gravity.

Using this technique, researchers from the University of California, Berkeley, found one of the planets around a star called Gliese 436. The planet appears to be

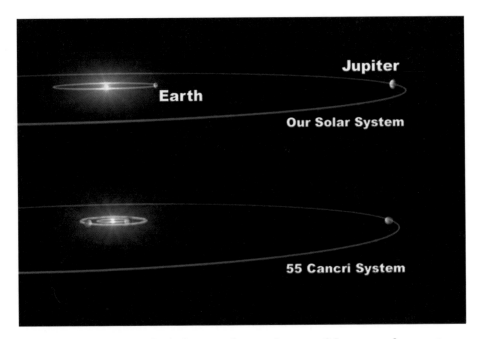

Figure 3.1 Among the planets that exist outside our solar system is a large planet—18 times bigger than Earth—that moves around the star called 55 Cancri. This diagram shows the orbit of 55 Cancri's planets as compared to that of Earth and Jupiter in our own solar system.

between 21 and 25 times the size of Earth. It speeds around its planet once every 2.64 days.

The second planet orbits a star called 55 Cancri, which is similar to the sun (Figure 3.1). It's probably 18 times the mass of Earth, and its "year" is just 2.81 days long, say researchers from the University of Texas in Austin. Their discovery adds to three Jupiter-size planets already known to orbit the same star.

The third planet, detected by astronomers in Portugal, is at least 14 times as massive as Earth. It orbits a star called mu Arae. Because the new planets are so small and close to their stars, astronomers suspect that the planets are rocky.

The discoveries may help astronomers figure out how planets form. And with Earth-like planets within our reach, the chances of finding life outside our solar system have improved a bit. Someone might be out there, after all.

Going Deeper:

Cowen, Ron. "Rocky Road: Planet Hunting Gets Closer to Earth." *Science News* 166 (September 4, 2004): 147. Available online at *http://www.sciencenews.org/articles/20040904/fob1.asp*.

Cousin Earth

by Emily Sohn

As their search continues, astronomers are finding more and more planets orbiting nearby stars. This time, they've detected a solid planet that's just 15 light-years from Earth.

Many details about the planet remain unknown because the astronomers didn't see it directly. Instead, they were able to detect how the planet's gravity makes its star wobble a little bit.

Out of 156 planets discovered so far in other solar systems, the new extrasolar planet is the smallest one yet found. It's about 7.5 times heavier than Earth.

Along with two, much bigger planets, the new world orbits a star called Gliese 876. The planet takes just 1.9 days to complete an orbit around Gliese 876. So, its year is much, much shorter than ours. It's so close to its star that its surface is hot enough to roast a chicken.

Most extrasolar planets that have been found so far are big balls of gas, like Jupiter and Saturn. Because the planet's mass is low, it probably couldn't hold onto much gas. So, scientists suspect that it's rocky.

"This could be the first [known] rocky planet around any normal star other than the sun," says team member

Jack Lissauer of NASA's Ames Research Center in Mountain View, California.

Scientists are still trying to figure out how rocky planets might form so close to their stars.

Whatever the answer, the new discovery gives researchers confidence that they will one day find even closer cousins to Earth somewhere in the universe. And, on a planet resembling Earth, they might also discover traces of life as we know it.

Going Deeper:

Cowen, Ron. "Planet Hunt Strikes Rock: Hot Kin of Earth Orbits Nearby Star." *Science News* 167 (June 18, 2005): 387. Available online at *http://www.sciencenews.org/articles/20050618/fob1.asp*.

You can learn more about the discovery of the planet orbiting Gliese 876 online at *http://www.nsf.gov/news/news_summ.jsp?cntn_id=104243&org=NSF*.

Exploring Our Solar System

Although scientists are always searching the galaxies outside our solar system for new planets that may contain traces of life, they also continue their exploration of our own solar system. For decades, most of us have accepted the idea that there are nine planets in our solar system as fact. According to new research, though, it is possible that there are other planets—like Sedna, for example—that might deserve to be part of the list. In the next article, author Emily Sohn examines the ongoing search for planets and other interesting objects that make up the solar system we call home.

—The Editor

Planets on the Edge

by Emily Sohn

Before Reading:

- **Name all the planets in our solar system.**

- **Have you ever looked through a telescope at the night sky? If you have, describe your experience.**

My Very Educated Mother Just Served Us Nine Pizzas.

Many kids use this short sentence (or something like it) to remember the names of the planets in order of their distance from the sun. The first letter of each word stands for a planet: Mercury, Venus, Earth, Mars, Jupiter, Saturn, Uranus, Neptune, Pluto.

But the solar system isn't quite this simple. The more deeply astronomers look into the sky, the more mysterious and complicated our neighborhood becomes.

Besides the nine planets (and not everyone agrees that Pluto is truly a planet), at least two rings of chunky dust, ice, and rock orbit the sun. The **asteroid belt** sits between Mars and Jupiter. Another ring, called the **Kuiper belt**, hovers way out where Pluto orbits.

Surprises keep popping up in the remotest parts of the solar system. In March 2004, astronomers from the California Institute of Technology announced that they had spotted a planet like object even farther out than Pluto. Such discoveries are forcing scientists to revise their ideas about how planets form.

FRINGE PLANETOID

The newly found object is named Sedna (Figure 3.2). It's about three-quarters the size of Pluto.

Is it a true planet? It orbits the sun, but some astronomers say that even Pluto is too small to be called a planet. So, many researchers describe Sedna as a **planetoid**.

- **What is a planetoid?**

Sedna orbits in the coldest, most distant parts of the solar system, where temperatures drop to –240 degrees Celsius [–400°F]. This coldness accounts for its name. Sedna is an Inuit goddess who lives in a frigid cave deep in the Arctic Ocean.

Sedna looks funny, too. It's bright red, like Mars. It's also shiny. Other highly reflective planets are covered with ice, but Sedna doesn't appear to have an icy surface. It may even have its own little moon.

- **Where did the name "Sedna" come from?**

And its orbit is wild. It takes more

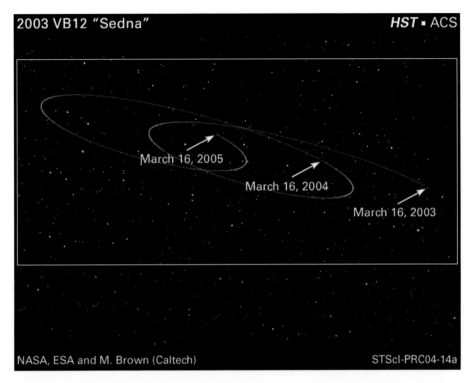

2003 VB12 "Sedna"   *HST* ▪ ACS

March 16, 2005

March 16, 2004

March 16, 2003

NASA, ESA and M. Brown (Caltech)   STScI-PRC04-14a

Figure 3.2 Some astronomers believe that Sedna, whose orbit is seen here, should be added to the official list of planets in our solar system.

than 10,500 years for Sedna to go once around the sun, following a very stretched-out path. Sometimes, it's as close to the sun as 75 times the distance from the sun to Earth. At other times, it can be as far away as about 1,000 times the distance from the sun to Earth. The other planets have orbits that are much closer to circular.

"One of the questions is why Sedna has this crazy orbit," says astronomer David Trilling of the University of Pennsylvania. "How did it get out there so far?"

CLOUD OR BELT?

Sedna's discoverers suggest that the planetoid belongs to a distant collection of icy objects known as the **Oort cloud**. More than 50 years ago, astronomers had predicted the existence of such a cloud at the edge of the solar system to account for certain kinds of comets that travel in enormous orbits that extend far beyond Pluto. Sedna may be the first sighting of an object belonging to this cloud.

Name the Eleventh Planet

My Very Educated Mother Just Served Us Nine Pizzas.

Many people use this short sentence (or something like it) to remember the names of the planets in order of their distance from the sun. The first letter of each word stands for a planet: Mercury, Venus, Earth, Mars, Jupiter, Saturn, Uranus, Neptune, Pluto.

Suppose that the newly discovered planetoid named Sedna counts as the tenth planet in the solar system and that you have just found another large, mysterious object even farther out than Sedna.

What name would you give to this 11th member of the solar system's family of planets? Notice that planet names tend to be the names of gods in ancient mythology.

Make up an 11-word sentence that gives the names of these 11 planets in order of their distance from the sun.

Other astronomers aren't so sure. They say that Sedna, like Pluto, belongs to the Kuiper belt. Sedna's size, 1700 kilometers (or about 1,000 miles) across, makes it too big to belong to the Oort cloud, they argue. And there are known objects in the Kuiper belt that have orbits farther out than that of Sedna.

• **What is the difference between the Oort cloud and the Kuiper belt?**

If astronomers can find more objects like Sedna, they may get a better understanding of how planets form and even how life began on Earth.

"If there is only one of these guys, you can pretty much make up any explanation you want," Trilling says. "But if this Sedna guy is the tip of the iceberg for a whole bunch of other guys like it, maybe we're missing something essential about how these guys formed."

Theorists suggest that the formation of big planets, such as Jupiter, sent leftover material to the outskirts of the solar system billions of years ago. Icy comets later wandering in from these frigid regions may have delivered the first drops of water to Earth, Mars, and other planets.

Getting a sense of how many objects are out there, how many used to be out there, and how they move could help astronomers refine their theories. Such observations could also improve predictions about the likelihood of an asteroid or comet hitting Earth.

A CLOSER LOOK

To get a better idea of what's going on, astronomers are taking a closer look at the Kuiper belt.

Some use ground telescopes to do enormous surveys of much of the sky. Robotic telescopes and computer programs analyze picture after picture until they detect slight movements of objects against the background of stars. This movement suggests the object belongs in the solar system. If anything interesting comes up, people take over the analysis. That's how the Caltech researchers found Sedna.

Other scientists take a more focused approach. In one recent project, University of Pennsylvania astronomers used the Hubble Space Telescope to take a long, hard look at one tiny portion of the Kuiper belt. Their scan covered just one two-millionth of the sky. Their goal was to identify as many of the smallest, faintest objects as possible.

Because the Kuiper belt is so far away, the smallest objects the Hubble Space Telescope can detect are 20 kilometers [12.4 miles] across—about the diameter of Philadelphia. This may sound big, Trilling says, but the most powerful telescopes on the ground can only catch objects 100 times as big.

For a week and a half, the Penn team took pictures using the Hubble and stared at them around the clock. "When I close my eyes after doing this all day or all night, I see stars," Trilling says. It's as if he's been punched, he says, "over and over again."

Theorists had predicted that this particular region of the Kuiper belt would have about 85 small objects in it. At the end of the study, however, the astronomers turned up only three.

"One of our conclusions was that collisions among [Kuiper belt objects] must have occurred more often than previously suspected," Trilling says. That would mean there are many more, really small objects that astronomers can't see yet.

- **What are the difficulties of spotting objects in the Kuiper belt?**

Lead researcher Gary Bernstein wants to do the same experiment again with another part of the Kuiper belt. He wants to make sure that the team didn't happen to pick an unusual part of the belt.

Unfortunately, so many astronomers have projects that it's hard to get time on the Hubble Space Telescope. The time pressure is even greater now that the National Aeronautics and Space Administration [NASA] has decided to retire the telescope.

If you want a better look at the fringes of the solar system, you

- **How do astronomers account for the fact that they found fewer objects in the Kuiper belt than they expected to find?**

- **How might the launch of the New Horizons spacecraft help research on the Kuiper belt?**

might have to wait another decade or two. NASA has plans to launch a spacecraft called New Horizons that will go to Pluto and beyond.

New Horizons is scheduled for launch in January 2006. It would swing past Jupiter to use that planet's gravity to boost its speed. Scientific studies would begin in February 2007. The spacecraft would reach Pluto and its moon, Charon, in July 2015. It would then head deeper into the Kuiper belt to study one or more of the icy objects in that vast region.

From past experience, astronomers suspect that there'll be lots more surprises.

After Reading:

- How does research on other planets help us understand Earth's formation and history?

- What might account for Sedna's strange orbit?

- The article says that, if Sedna is unusual or an exception, its discovery may not contribute much to increasing our understanding of the solar system. However, if there are many objects like Sedna, scientists are missing "something essential." Explain why finding a one-of-a-kind object might not be as helpful as finding lots of similar objects.

- Make an argument why NASA should or should not retire the Hubble Space Telescope.

A Very Old Planet

In 2003, astronomers made a very exciting discovery. They found a far-off planet that may be about 12.5 billion years old. If their findings are correct, then this planet was created when the universe itself was still young, and may be able to provide scientists with important information about how the universe was formed. In the next article, author Emily Sohn describes this recently found planet and what its advanced age means for the future of space science.

—The Editor

A Planet From the Early Universe

by Emily Sohn

If you thought your parents were old, get this.

Astronomers have discovered the oldest and most distant planet known in the universe (Figure 3.3). The planet is so far away that it takes light 7,200 years to get here from there.

The new discovery is full of surprises. For one thing, scientists found it deep inside a dense cluster of stars called M4, which is about 12.5 billion years old. This means the planet itself is about that old, so it formed when the universe was just a baby.

Most planets found so far outside of our solar system orbit much younger stars. Our own sun and Earth are just under 5 billion years old. The new finding suggests that planets may have formed soon after the universe started, much earlier than scientists used to think.

To detect the new planet, Steinn Sigurdsson of Pennsylvania State University and his colleagues used observations from the Hubble Space Telescope and from a telescope on Earth that detects radio waves.

After comparing data from both sources, the researchers concluded that the new planet weighs 2.5

Figure 3.3 This NASA photograph provides a view of what is believed to be the oldest planet in the universe.

times as much as Jupiter. It orbits two stars at about the distance that Uranus orbits our sun.

Astronomers can now start looking for other planets in distant, old star clusters like M4. Maybe you can teach an old star new tricks!

Going Deeper:

Cowen, Ron. "Record Breaker: A Planet From the Early Universe." *Science News* 164 (July 12, 2003): 19. Available online at *http://www.sciencenews.org/20030712/fob1.asp*.

The Dust of Outer Space

Scientists know that outer space is full of lots of things—
stars, comets, asteroids, and, perhaps most abundant of
all: dust. The way dust gathers in the universe helps
astronomers determine what other objects lie nearby,
like planets. In the next article, writer Emily Sohn
describes the way "space dust" plays a pivotal role in
helping scientists discover new celestial objects.

—The Editor

A Dusty Birthplace

by Emily Sohn

Outer space is a messy place. Besides all the asteroids, comets, and planets floating around, disks of dust particles surround many young stars.

A recent analysis is revealing new information about one particularly famous dust disk. This disk hovers around a star called Beta Pictoris. The research points to a possible planet orbiting the star, plus a collection of asteroids and comets.

Scientists have known about the dusty disk around Beta Pictoris for 20 years. Many details, though, have long been missing.

The dust that often surrounds young stars comes from all the action that happens nearby, as planets, asteroids, and comets form and then slam into each other.

To learn what the dust around Beta Pictoris is made of, astronomers from Japan used an infrared camera on a telescope in Hawaii. The images showed three distinct bands of tiny dust particles.

To describe how far these bands are from the star, the scientists used a distance measurement called an astronomical unit (AU). One AU is equal to the distance between the sun and Earth.

Around Beta Pictoris, the closest band of dust is 6.4 AU from the star. The other two bands lie at distances of 16 and 30 AU.

Normally, it would take less than 100 years for the tiny dust particles to be blown away into space. The fact that the disk around Beta Pictoris is still present suggests that some process is constantly restocking the particles that make up the bands, the scientists say. One possibility is collisions between asteroids.

There might also be a planet at a distance of 12 AU from the star, the data suggest. That's just slightly greater than Saturn's distance from the sun. This planet's gravity could be helping to keep the dust belts from flying away into space and dispersing.

Further studies may provide additional details about how objects in the universe form and change. Tidiness probably has nothing to do with it!

Going Deeper:

Cowen, Ron. "Planet Signs? Sifting a Dusty Disk." *Science News* **166 (October 9, 2004): 227–228. Available online at** *http://www.sciencenews.org/ articles/20041009/fob2.asp*.

A Melting Planet

Earlier, we mentioned that celestial bodies have a limit to how big they can get. Like stars, planets seem to have ways to keep their size consistent. As Emily Sohn demonstrates in the following article, the orbit of one planet takes it so close to its star that it essentially "melts" a little bit each time it passes. Over time, this melting seems to help the planet "slim down."

—The Editor

A Planet's Slim-Fast Plan

by Emily Sohn

If you sit in a parked car on a hot summer's day, you may feel like you're melting. But that's nothing compared to what some planets go through.

Scientists have been studying a planet called HD209458b, which orbits precariously close to its star. The star itself is about 150 light years from Earth. HD209458b is one-eighth the distance from its sun as Mercury is from ours.

New observations of HD209458b suggest that brutal gusts of heat and radiation along with strong tugs of gravity from its star may be too much for the planet to bear. Every second, in fact, 10,000 tons of hydrogen gas get blasted off of HD209458b, Alfred Vidal-Madfar of the Astrophysics Institute of Paris and his colleagues report.

At that rate, the planet will probably still be okay. Weighing in at 70% the mass of Jupiter, HD209458b has lost only 0.1% of its mass since its birth 5 billion years ago.

But the findings suggest that other planets which orbit even closer to their stars might evaporate completely. That could help explain why scientists have found so few planets with super-tight orbits outside the solar system.

As scientists continue to learn more about the atmosphere of HD209458b, one question lingers: When will they come up with a name for the planet that's easier to remember?

Going Deeper:

Cowen, Ron. "Planet's Slim-fast Plan: Extrasolar Orb Is Too Close for Comfort." *Science News* 163 (March 15, 2003): 164. Available online at *http://www.sciencenews.org/20030315/fob3.asp*.

Section 4

Exploring Mars

If you've been paying attention to the news in recent years, you can't possibly have missed hearing something about the planet Mars. The Red Planet, as Mars is known, has a fiery appearance due to the rust that lies on its surface (opposite).

As the fourth planet from the Sun and one of the planets most similar to Earth in composition, Mars is of great interest to scientists—especially those who are searching for evidence that life exists, or has existed in the past, on planets other than Earth.

For the past few years, technologically advanced space rovers have been roaming the surface of Mars, collecting data and samples of soil and atmosphere and taking spectacular photographs that are beamed back to Earth for scientists to study. From these investigations, it has become clear that water once flowed on Martian soil, which means life likely existed there, too. In this section, we follow the path of the Mars rovers and the satellites that have been sent into space to collect information about the mysteries of the Red Planet.

—The Editor

Traveling to Mars

Maybe you've dreamed of being able to travel into outer space someday. If so, you've likely wondered whether people would ever be able to set foot on Mars—the mysterious Red Planet. We've already sent robots there to explore the surface, and scientists are learning more about Mars and its history every day. In the following article, author Emily Sohn examines the obstacles that still need to be overcome before people can think seriously about traveling to Mars.

—The Editor

Destination Mars

by Emily Sohn

Before Reading:

• **Why has Mars been in the news lately?**

• **Name four facts about Mars.**

If you're lucky, you might someday walk on the surface of Mars.

For some scientists, the question is no longer whether people will ever get to Mars. It's a question of when people will travel there. The most cautious of the bunch say it may take many decades to overcome the obstacles standing in the way of such an expedition. Others are more optimistic.

"I'd like to think that missions will be going there as early as 15 years from now," says Paul Wooster. He's director of the Mars Gravity Biosatellite Program at the Massachusetts Institute of Technology (MIT).

Whether or not you want to go to Mars yourself, the Red Planet is exciting. Two radio-controlled robots, named *Spirit* and *Opportunity*, are now exploring the

• **Who is Paul Wooster?**

planet. The rovers are sending back amazing images and information about places that scientists had never before studied in such detail.

Meanwhile, in 2004, President George W. Bush proposed giving the National Aeronautics and Space Administration (NASA) $12 billion over the next five years for space exploration. He committed the United States to the goal of getting astronauts back to the moon by 2020 and then going beyond.

- What are *Spirit* and *Opportunity*, and what are they doing?

"We do not know where this journey will end, yet we know this: Human beings are headed into the cosmos," President Bush said in January 2004.

MICE IN SPACE

Before any of us can vacation on Mars, though, there are still plenty of complications to iron out. Some of the biggest questions have to do with the human body. We are fine-tuned to deal with conditions here on Earth. How our bodies might react to living on another planet is anybody's guess.

Gravity, in particular, is a big concern. Because Mars is smaller and less massive than Earth, its gravity is weaker than Earth's. A person weighing 100 pounds [45 kg] on Earth would weigh just 38 pounds [17 kg] on

Mars. What's more, astronauts would experience **zero gravity** during the year or more of travel time going to and from Mars.

When astronauts spend time in zero gravity, their muscles and bones break down. It's as if they had been lying motionless in bed for a long time. If astronauts don't do weight-bearing exercises while they're in orbit aboard the space shuttle or space station, it can be difficult for them to walk when they get back. The longer astronauts spend in space, the longer it takes them to recover.

> • What problems do scientists have to overcome for astronauts to survive on Mars?

A mission to Mars would last at least two and a half years, including travel time. That's much longer than anyone has previously spent in outer space.

To find out how mammals might fare on Mars, Wooster is planning to send 15 mice into outer space. Each mouse will have its own cage. For five weeks, the spacecraft will spin just enough for the mice to experience the gravitational pull found on Mars.

Over the course of the mission, Wooster and his collaborators (which include more than 100 college students around the world) will monitor the health and activity levels of the mice.

> • How long would a trip to Mars take?

Each cage will be built to collect urine samples on cloth pads underneath a mesh barrier at the bottom of the cage. Every few days, an automated system will roll up and store the urine-soaked pads. When the mission returns to Earth, the scientists will look at chemical markers in the urine to measure how quickly muscles and bones break down.

"This is going to be the longest, partial-gravity study on mammals in space," says Wooster, who hopes to launch the mission as early as 2006.

What happens to mice could also happen to people. The data that researchers collect will help determine how much exercise and what types of activity Mars travelers might need to stay healthy and strong for the entire trip.

And there are other complications.

Mars doesn't have any grocery stores or fast-food restaurants. Plants don't even grow there. And the rovers still haven't found pools of liquid water on the planet. So, astronauts will have to bring all their food and water with them—enough to last several years.

Also, it will be impossible for people to breathe Martian air, which is 95% carbon dioxide. Earth's atmosphere is 78% nitrogen, 21% oxygen, and about 0.035% carbon dioxide. Astronauts will need reliable spacesuits, pressurized vehicles, and airtight shelters to survive on Mars.

Heavily insulated clothes will also be essential. Because Mars is farther from the sun than Earth, it gets extremely cold in winter, with temperatures as low as –111 degrees Celsius [-167.8°F]. And a Martian year lasts 687 Earth days.

PLANETARY RESEARCH

Putting people on Mars would be a huge boost for planetary research, Wooster says.

• **How long is a Martian year?**

"In a couple of hours at most, an astronaut can do pretty much everything the rovers there are doing currently," he says. "And an astronaut can do it much better and more comprehensively."

Already, *Spirit* and *Opportunity* have turned up some interesting findings about the rocks, dirt, and landscape of Mars. *Opportunity*, for instance, dug a trench with its front wheel. Analyses showed that the soil composition changes with depth. The way the soil is packed together suggests the presence of small amounts of water in the past.

On the other side of the planet, *Spirit* found the top layer of soil to be stickier than expected. One possibility is that liquid water in the soil that was once present in the soil combined with salts to produce the stickiness.

Finding water on Mars would be an enormous tri-

Figure 4.1 **The landscape of Mars is rough and full of features you might recognize from Earth, like this volcano—called Olympus Mons.**

umph. Water makes life possible here on Earth. So, finding signs of water on Mars would indicate that life might have existed there in the past and could still lurk there today.

Today, mobile robots are exploring Mars. In a few years, mice may experience Mars in their own way. Looking farther ahead, you might be the one who gets to stroll across the Red Planet's dusty surface (Figure 4.1).

- **What have *Spirit* and *Opportunity* found that could suggest life once existed or still may lurk on Mars?**

After Reading:

- **If life exists somewhere in the solar system other than Earth, why is Mars a good candidate?**

- **Do you approve of President Bush's pledge to fund space exploration, including a base on the moon and a trip to Mars? Why or why not?**

- **Do you think President Bush's goal of "getting astronauts back to the moon by 2020 and then going beyond" is realistic? Where do you think "beyond" should be?**

- **Besides the physical strains of living on Mars, what other strains and difficulties might astronauts on the planet face?**

- **What would you like the rovers now on Mars to look for or at? Why?**

Mars Rovers

In 2003, the National Aeronautics and Space Administration (NASA) landed two robot-controlled rovers, called *Spirit* and *Opportunity*, on the surface of the planet Mars. In the years since they arrived, the twin rovers have been working hard, taking photographs of the Martian landscape and collecting samples of soil and atmosphere that scientists will be able to study later. In the next article, author Sorcha McDonagh examines the exciting findings made by NASA's amazing Mars rovers.

—The Editor

Roving the Red Planet

by Sorcha McDonagh

This little robot is a long way from home. *Spirit*, a remote-controlled rover with six chunky wheels, made its first outing on Mars in January 2004. But *Spirit* has gotten into trouble. It lost contact with scientists back on Earth for a while and suffered various computer glitches. Although mission scientists are making repairs, they're not sure whether they can get *Spirit* back to full working order.

Still, the rover did get some tasks done before malfunctioning. *Spirit*'s landing site is in a large crater known as Gusev. Scientists suspect that the crater may have once held a massive lake. *Spirit*'s job is to search for evidence of this lake in the crater's rocks and soil. The rover carries different types of tools for making these investigations, some of which are mounted on an extendable arm. Among the tools are two **spectrometers**—devices used to analyze the chemical makeup of an object or substance.

Spirit first used its spectrometers to study rocks and soil just 3 meters [9.8 feet] from its landing site. It found that the soil is rich in the elements chlorine, sulfur, silicon, and iron. The soil's composition is similar to that of soil analyzed previously at three other Martian landing

The Martian Games

People enjoy sports, which provide much needed exercise as well as entertainment. But what sports could be played on Mars? Do a bit of research on what Mars is like. What games do you like to play on Earth that you could play on Mars? Would you have to change anything about that game?

Challenge: Pick a sport (or create one of your own) and make whatever changes you think would be necessary so that the sport can be part of the First Martian Games.

Consider the terrain of Mars.
Consider the gravity of Mars.
Consider temperature and other factors.
Consider the suits and other equipment
   required on Mars.

Tell us about your Martian sport in a drawing, a list of rules, or by writing a short paragraph describing how it is played.

sites, says lead scientist Steve Squyres of Cornell University.

Spirit also found the first traces of nickel and zinc on Mars. And it detected a mineral called **olivine**—usually found in volcanic rock on Earth.

Scientists have long known that Mars is dotted with long extinct volcanoes, such as the Olympus Mons, the

| Apron Covering Dunes | Apron on Polygons | Fresh, Dust-free Surfaces |

437 yd
400 m

164 yd
150 m

164 yd
150 m

Figure 4.2 The Mars rovers have discovered traces like these of sites where water once flowed on the surface of the planet.

largest volcano in the solar system. But the discovery of olivine also provides clues about the presence of water at the Gusev crater (Figure 4.2).

Harry Y. McSween of the University of Tennessee says that olivine quickly changes into different compounds when water is present. Because there's still olivine at the Gusev crater, this could mean that there was never water at the site. Or it could be that the soil formed long after an ancient lake disappeared.

Squyres believes that lake sediments exist somewhere deep in the crater's soil. He's just not sure how far down they may be.

Mission scientists are working hard to fix *Spirit*. In the meantime, its sibling rover, *Opportunity*, is getting ready to wheel around on the opposite side of Mars—and taking some of the best pictures of Martian rock formations yet seen.

Going Deeper:

Cowen, Ron. "Spirit Gets Its Wheels Dirty: Mars Rover Begins Scientific Work." *Science News* 165 (January 24, 2004): 51–52. Available online at *http://www.sciencenews.org/20040124/fob2.asp*.

Section 5

The Stuff of the Universe

The universe, simply defined, is made up of everything that exists—space, planets, stars, comets, asteroids, and even us. Earlier in this book, we looked at several of the components of the universe, including galaxies, planets, and stars. Now we turn to some of the lesser known—and often more interesting—aspects of the universe, from black holes to antimatter.

Most scientists believe the universe began about 14 billion years ago, with a massive explosion called the **Big Bang**. Since then, it has been expanding in every direction as it continues to form new planets, stars, and other celestial objects. Astronomers argue over the ultimate fate of the universe. Some think it will keep expanding forever, while others believe it will someday collapse into itself in a sort of reverse Big Bang. While scientists debate the future of the universe, they also explore its features.

In the first article, we look at the phenomenon of "dark matter," the invisible material that lies between stars and other bodies in space and actually forms the bulk of the universe. The second article describes black holes—those mysterious space features that seem to "suck" anything in their path inside themselves. Next, we examine some strange icy objects that have been found at the edge of our solar system, Then we look at how explosions can occur in space and how they affect the universe. Finally, we discuss the strange issue of antimatter, which seems to exist as an opposing force to all the "stuff" of the universe.

—The Editor

Dark Matter

If someone asked you to describe what lies between the
stars and planets, could you it? You might say it's just
"space," but that wouldn't be entirely accurate. In the next
article, author Emily Sohn explains that the darkness
between celestial objects actually has substance. It's
called dark matter or dark energy, and scientists are studying it to learn more about the makeup of the universe.

—The Editor

Strange Universe: The Stuff of Darkness

by Emily Sohn

Before Reading:

- **What is matter?**

- **What do you think might lie hidden in the darkness between stars?**

- **Name three things studied by scientists that your eye can't see directly.**

It isn't easy to study darkness.

Try it. Next time you're outside on a clear night, look up. You might see the winking lights of an airplane, the glow of an orbiting satellite, or even the bright trail of a meteor. Of course, you'll see lots of stars.

What about all the space between the stars? Is something hidden out there in the darkness? Or is it merely empty?

There's nothing for the human eye to see, but astronomers are finding ways to detect what lies between the stars. And they're discovering that most of the universe is made out of mysterious, invisible stuff. They call it **dark matter** and **dark energy**.

Although they can't see it directly, scientists are pretty sure this weird stuff exists. Figuring out exactly what it is, however, remains a work in progress.

"We're just now beginning to peel away the darkness," says Robert Kirshner, an astronomer at Harvard University. "We're beginning to see what things are really like, and it's a funny, very unsettling picture because it's so new and unfamiliar."

ORDINARY MATTER

When you look around, everything you see is a type of matter. This is the ordinary stuff of the universe, from a grain of salt to a drop of water to a candy bar. You are matter. So is Earth, the moon, the sun, and our own Milky Way galaxy.

Simple enough, right? Until about 1970, our picture of the universe seemed this straightforward. But then Jeremiah Ostriker of Princeton University and other astronomers started to notice something curious.

Gravity provided the hint. The force of gravity keeps us stuck to the ground, the moon in orbit around Earth, and Earth in orbit around the sun. Without gravity, these bodies would fly off on their own.

In general, the force of gravity between any two objects depends on the distance between them and on the amount of **matter**, or **mass**, in each object. The sun, for example, contains a lot more matter than Earth, so it has a much larger mass and exerts a much greater gravitational force than Earth.

Astronomers can estimate how much ordinary, visible matter a star or a galaxy contains. They can then figure out how the gravity of, for example, one galaxy would affect another, nearby galaxy.

- **Explain why the force of gravity of the sun is greater than the force of gravity of a car.**

When astronomers compared their calculations to what really happens in our own galaxy, they were surprised to find that the Milky Way acts as if it has much more mass than it should. It's like going to the carnival where someone tries to guess your weight from your appearance and finds that you weigh 1,000 pounds [454 kg] instead of 100 pounds [45.4 kg] when you step on the scale.

Measurements of other galaxies produced the same puzzling result.

- **If dark matter can't be seen, how do we know that it might exist?**

OUT OF DARKNESS

The only logical conclusion, Ostriker says, was that there's lots of stuff out there that's invisible yet still has mass. Scientists named it "dark matter." Ordinary matter can give off or reflect light; dark matter does not.

Even then, the concept was too baffling for many

> • **What is the difference between ordinary matter and dark matter?**

people to believe at first, Ostriker says. "But every measurement you make gives the same answer," he says. "Now, we have to believe it."

Indeed, calculations show that there may be 10 times as much dark matter as ordinary matter in the universe. The part we see is only a small fraction of all the stuff in the universe.

So what is dark matter? "We have no more clue now than we did 30 years ago," Ostriker says.

Scientists have been trying out all sorts of ideas. One idea is that dark matter is made of teeny-tiny particles that give off no light, so they can't be detected by telescopes. But it's hard to decide what sort of particle fits the bill.

"Right now it's a lot of guesses, and it's highly uncertain," Ostriker says.

Astronomers need more help to figure out what dark matter is. You might end up working on this puzzle yourself if you study astronomy or physics. And if that puzzle isn't challenging enough for you, there's more.

ANOTHER FORCE

Once astronomers accepted the idea of dark matter, another mystery turned up.

According to the Big Bang theory, the universe started with a huge explosion that pushed all the stars and galaxies away from each other. Based on their measurements of matter and dark matter, scientists concluded that gravity should eventually reverse this motion. It would make the universe collapse back in on itself billions of years from now.

It came as a huge surprise, then, when powerful telescope observations revealed that just the opposite seems to be happening. By measuring and analyzing light from distant exploding stars called **supernovas**, astronomers discovered that it looks as if the universe is expanding outward faster and faster.

This shocking discovery suggests that the universe has some sort of additional force that pushes stars and galaxies apart, countering gravity. And the effect of this mysterious force must be larger than that of all the matter and dark matter in the universe. For lack of a better name, scientists call this effect "dark energy."

So, the bulk of the universe is not stars and galaxies and planets and people. Most of the universe is other stuff. And a lot of this other stuff is something very strange called dark energy.

- What problem did scientists discover with the Big Bang theory?

"Now that's a really weird picture," Kirshner says. "In a way, you could say that in the last five years, we've

- **Explain the difference between dark matter and dark energy.**

stumbled into two-thirds of the universe."

Researchers are now hard at work, using telescopes on the ground and in space to look for clues that would tell them more about dark matter and dark energy.

ANOTHER VIEW

What's the point of studying stuff that we can't even see?

Just thinking about dark matter and dark energy separates us from other animals, Ostriker says. "When you pick up a rock and see little creatures scurrying around, you can say, 'What do they know about life except what's under that rock?'" We, on the other hand, can try to understand the universe outside of us, he says.

That can give us a new perspective, Kirshner says.

- **What does astronomer Robert Kirshner mean when he says, "We're just now beginning to peel away the darkness"?**

We can take pleasure in the fact that we're made from a very small minority of the kinds of stuff that exist in the universe, he says. Studying dark matter and dark energy gives us a sense of how valuable and unusual this "ordinary" sort of matter is.

So, there's a lot more to darkness than meets the eye, and it's worth taking a closer look.

After Reading:

- If you were interested in learning more about dark matter or dark energy, where would you look? Name three resources for further inquiry.

- Why do scientists think the universe is expanding?

- Dark matter is still very mysterious stuff. Describe some of the candidates for what dark matter might be.

SCIENCE
NEWS for
KIDS

Going Inside a Black Hole

Have you ever lost something and said it must have disappeared into a black hole? We've all heard of black holes and even have some idea of how their massive gravitational pull "sucks" in other celestial objects. In the following article, author Emily Sohn takes us on a dangerous and exciting journey right inside a black hole—one of the most fearsome and mysterious things in the universe.

—The Editor

Black Hole Journey

by Emily Sohn

Before Reading:

- **List what you know about black holes.**

- **What is a supernova?**

There are all sorts of holes: big ones and little ones, deep ones and shallow ones. There are swimming holes and buttonholes, cheese holes and bullet holes. Then, there are **black holes**.

These mysterious, bizarre objects pack a huge mass into a tiny volume. Their gravity is so strong that they gobble up anything that comes near them, even stars, gas, and light. They're invisible. They're like cracks in space, and they lurk all over the universe.

If you were to jump into a black hole (something that no one has yet figured out how to do), you'd be stretched from head to toe and squeezed from side to side into a long string of human spaghetti. Finally, you'd get pulverized into the tiniest bits imaginable.

"If you were to fall in, what remains of you would eventually come out as light and other particles," says

Tom Banks. He's a physicist who spends a lot of his time thinking about black holes and trying to understand them.

"There wouldn't be much of you that we could recognize," Banks says. "It would be as if we had burned you up in a fire. Everything in the body would come out as nothing more than radiation and ashes."

• **What would happen if you jumped into a black hole?**

Both scientists and nonscientists find black holes fascinating. The whole idea sounds crazy, and it can be hard to wrap your head around something that seems like it should be impossible. Nevertheless, new observations and thought experiments are shining light into the darkness.

Astronomers now suspect that there's a black hole at the center of just about every galaxy in the universe (Figure 5.1). Some researchers even suggest that the universe was once a big ball of black holes, before there were any stars or planets.

Further research on black holes might eventually help explain how the universe began, Banks says. He works at Rutgers University in New Brunswick, New Jersey, and at the University of California, Santa Cruz.

"One of the questions we ask ourselves is, 'What happened in the very, very earliest moments of the universe?'" he says.

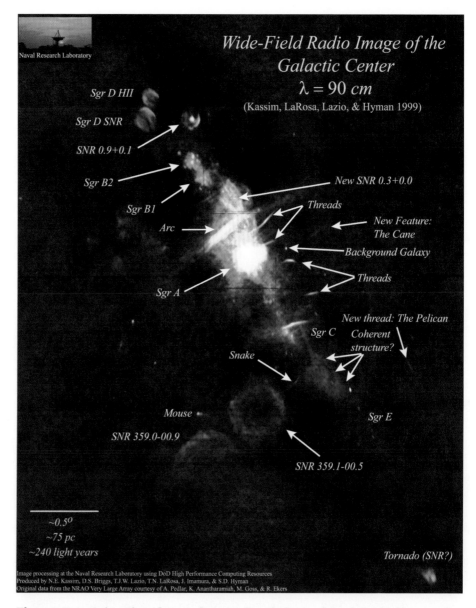

Figure 5.1 Scientists have determined that a black hole lies at the center of our Milky Way galaxy. This diagram shows where the black hole is located, labeled "The Cane."

SUPERNOVAS AND GRAVITY

A century ago, Albert Einstein's theory of gravitation predicted that black holes might exist. But no one wanted to believe it, including Einstein himself. Astronomers finally began to detect signs of black holes in the 1980s.

Scientists now are pretty sure that a black hole can form when a huge star reaches the end of its life and runs out of fuel. First, the inner part of the star collapses. Then there's an enormous explosion called a supernova, sending light and matter into space. Eventually, the entire mass of what's left of the star gets squeezed into the tiniest space imaginable—forming a black hole.

The more mass an object has, the more gravity it has. So, black holes have a lot of gravity. Black holes formed in a supernova may be only a few times the mass of our sun. On the other hand, black holes at the centers of galaxies may have a billion times as much mass as the sun, all crammed into a very small space.

- **Whose theory first predicted that black holes could exist?**

- **How are supernovas and black holes related?**

Earth's gravity keeps us on the ground; a black hole's gravity sucks things in. Its pull is so strong that not even light can escape. That's why it looks black—as if there's nothing there.

A black hole's size is defined by an invisible boundary called an event horizon. Anything—you, atoms, or light—that gets sucked in and crosses the boundary can never get back out again.

The more you think about black holes, the harder it is to imagine how they could possibly exist. That's what most interests many people, Banks says.

When he was a kid, Banks always wanted to know about extremes—the tallest building in the world, the deepest part of the ocean, the most of anything. "In that sense, black holes are the ultimate extreme," he says.

That's also what intrigues many scientists about black holes. "It's the ultimate limit on how much you can squeeze stuff together," Banks says. "This suggests that black holes tell us something about the fundamental theory of what matter or the universe looks like in its most extreme condition."

DATA AND THEORY

Because black holes are so weird (not to mention invisible), they can be difficult to study.

Scientists tackle this problem in two ways. Some use telescopes to make observations, staring into the sky and looking for signs of radiation that signal the presence of a black hole. Others use mathematics and computers to develop theories about black holes and explore the behavior of equations that describe such objects. They do thought experiments.

Theorists, such as Banks, look at data and try to understand observations made by astronomers. They attempt to put it all together to explain how the universe came to look the way it does now.

For example, astronomers observe many different kinds of galaxies. At the same time, theorists develop equations that link the shapes of galaxies to how they formed and evolved. Researchers can then compare what the formulas predict to what's actually seen in the sky.

"You continually go back and forth between observations and theory," Banks says. "If the theory doesn't work, you change it a little bit until you get something that works better."

This type of thinking has led some theorists to propose that entire galaxies can actually collapse into black holes.

A complicated set of ideas called "**string theory**" has also led some physicists to suggest that the universe once held a whole bunch of black holes, all scrunched together. Eventually, these black holes grew and separated, and each one formed a galaxy around itself. It's possible that every galaxy visible today has a massive black hole at its center.

- **What methods do scientists use to study black holes?**

But the equations developed so far by theorists provide only part of the picture. The rest is still a work in progress. With string theory and other ideas, scientists hope eventually to come up with a grand explanation for how everything came to be.

But, even if researchers do get all the numbers to work, black holes and the history of the universe might always remain something of a mystery.

"We weren't there at the beginning of the universe," Banks says. "We can't go look. We make theories to predict what we see today. We don't yet have a good enough theory to pin it all down."

Ready to jump in?

After Reading:

- Why do you think that scientists are so interested in learning about the beginning of the universe?

- How might scientists use math to study black holes? To get some idea, see *http://antwrp.gsfc.nasa.gov/htmltest/rjn_bht.html* (*NASA Goddard Space Flight Center*).

- Why do you think that many people, including Albert Einstein, for a long time supposed that black holes couldn't actually exist?

- Does the name "black hole" make sense? Come up with another (perhaps more logical) name that you could use for such an object.

- What might the universe have been like in its earliest moments? See *http://www.esa.int/esaKIDSen/SEMSZ5WJD1E_OurUniverse_0.html* (*European Space Agency*) or *http://www.worldalmanacforkids.com/explore/space/cosmology.html* (*World Almanac for Kids*).

What's in the Kuiper Belt?

The Kuiper belt, named after Dutch American astronomer Gerald Peter Kuiper (1905–1973), is a part of our solar system that reaches from within the orbit of Neptune toward the Sun. Inside it, lots of celestial bodies are in orbit. In fact, astronomers believe that many objects— including planets—originate there, as icy orbs. But recently, scientists have discovered that there are not as many things in the Kuiper belt as there once were. Where did they go? In the next article, writer Emily Sohn examines this mystery.

—The Editor

Icy Orbs at the Solar System's Edge

by Emily Sohn

Astronomers have to do lots of guesswork. They study many things that they can't see very well, so they have to make educated assumptions based on various clues and observations. Sometimes, those assumptions turn out to be wrong.

The Kuiper belt is a perfect example. This ring of objects sits way out on the edge of our solar system. Comets come out of it. The planet Pluto may be part of it. And scientists have long thought that the belt had a lot of big objects. Pluto, for instance, is 2,400 kilometers [1,491 miles] across. Plenty of other objects out there might be close to 1,000 kilometers [621 miles] across.

Or maybe not, says a group of researchers from the University of Arizona in Tucson. Their research now shows that many Kuiper belt objects may be much smaller than scientists previously thought.

Objects that are this small and far away can't be measured directly. Instead, astronomers usually estimate the size of a Kuiper belt object by how bright it is and how well its surface reflects light. Their calculations depend on the known connection between brightness and the size of comets that have supposedly left the belt and moved toward Earth.

New observations, however, show that Kuiper belt objects reflect light three times better than comets do. This means that the objects are much smaller than their brightness seemed to indicate. They may be only 60% of the size they were thought to be.

Suddenly, astronomers are confused about all sorts of things. One popular theory holds that there used to be a lot more stuff in the Kuiper belt than there is now, but no one knows where it all went. Now, there are even more missing objects to account for.

Going Deeper:

McDonagh, Sorcha. "Catching a Comet's Tail." *Science News for Kids* (January 14, 2004). Available online at *http://www.sciencenewsforkids.org/articles/20040114/Note2.asp*.

Shi ga, David. "Belt Tightening: Icy Orbs Are Surprisingly Small." *Science News* 166 (November 20, 2004): 326. Available online at *http://www.sciencenews.org/articles/20041120/fob7.asp*.

Sohn, Emily. "Saturn's New Moons." *Science News for Kids* (August 25, 2004). Available online at *http://www.sciencenewsforkids.org/articles/20040825/Note3.asp*.

You can learn more about the Kuiper belt online at *http://solarsystem.nasa.gov/planets/profile.cfm?Object=KBOs&Display=Kids*.

Space Explosions

In space, things tend to explode quite often. These explosions don't necessarily cause the same kind of damage they would here on Earth, but that doesn't mean space explosions have no effect. In fact, scientists can look at these explosions to find out more about how celestial objects form, as author Emily Sohn explains in the next article.

—The Editor

Burst Busters

by Emily Sohn

Explosions on Earth are a pretty big deal. In outer space, though, things are blowing up all the time. Two new studies show that a particularly powerful type of explosion is 10 times as common, but not always as powerful, as astronomers had thought.

The explosions are called gamma-ray bursts. One seems to appear whenever a dying star collapses and becomes a spinning black hole or **neutron star**. Particles burst out of a doughnut-shaped disk that surrounds the collapsed star, producing **gamma rays**.

A leading theory proposes that all gamma-ray bursts have the same amount of energy. In that case, the energy we detect here on Earth mostly depends on how far away the explosion is and how much of the blast is aimed in our direction.

New data cast doubt on that assumption. On December 3, 2003, a European satellite called INTE-GRAL recorded an unusual gamma-ray burst officially labeled GRB 031203. Two teams, one from Russia and one from California, looked closely at the data.

They found that the burst happened in a galaxy that is relatively close to us, just 1.3 billion light years away.

Oddly, though, it had only about one-thousandth as much energy as do bursts that come from much farther away. Analysis of the afterglow confirmed that the burst was a low-energy event.

Astronomers might be missing many gamma-ray bursts because they've been looking only for high-energy explosions, the researchers say. In October, the scheduled launch of a satellite called Swift might help resolve the issue. Swift is designed to register fainter bursts than telescopes on Earth normally detect.

Going Deeper:

Cowen, Ron. "Explosive News: Telescopes Find Signs of Gentler Gamma-ray Bursts." *Science News* 166 (August 7, 2004): 83–84. Available online at *http://www.sciencenews.org/articles/20040807/fob2.asp*.

SCIENCE
NEWS
for
KIDS

What Is Antimatter?

If you're interested in science fiction, you may have heard about the idea that every object or energy in the universe has an opposite somewhere out there. That is, matter has *antimatter*. This concept is not just science fiction. As author Emily Sohn demonstrates in the following article, antimatter is one of the most intriguing areas of study in the science of space and astronomy.

—The Editor

The Mirror Universe of Antimatter

by Emily Sohn

Before Reading:

- **What are the three main parts of an atom?**

- **What are some examples of matter?**

- **What is the Big Bang theory?**

Had a fight with your parents or a bad day at school? Wouldn't it be nice to step through a mirror to enter a different, yet somehow familiar world on the other side?

In some ways, this might not be such a farfetched idea. Physicists around the world are using high-tech machines to make particles of so-called **antimatter**. They think of antiparticles as mirror images of the particles that make up everything in our everyday world. Just as you look like your image in a mirror, except that right and left are interchanged, a particle and its antiparticle are identical, except that they have opposite electrical charges.

The research probably won't turn up anything exotic—certainly nothing like a galactic **wormhole** that would

- **What is antimatter?**

let you slip instantly from one part of the universe to another. Studying antimatter, however, could help scientists understand the origins and makeup of the universe. And particles of antimatter already play an important part in medical equipment used to scan the brain to monitor mental activity.

ORDINARY MATTER

Few people—and most of them are cutting-edge physicists—have ever seen antimatter (Figure 5.2). The rest of us are much more familiar with matter. Air, water, a table, the TV—you name it—everything we see, touch, eat, drink, and breathe is made up of tiny objects called atoms. Atoms, in turn, are made up of even tinier particles: electrons, protons, and neutrons.

Electrons have a negative electrical charge, and protons have a positive electrical charge. Neutrons have no electrical charge. A typical atom is made up of an equal number of electrons and protons, along with some neutrons. The number of protons in an atom determines what kind of atom it is. A hydrogen atom, for example, consists of just one proton and one electron.

Each type of particle has an elusive anti-partner. An antiproton is

• What is the difference between an electron and a proton? How is a positron different from each of these particles?

Apr 21 2002 02:29:35

Figure 5.2 This high-tech NASA photograph provides a rare glimpse of antimatter, seen as a green glowing orb at the center of the image.

just like a proton, except that it has a negative charge. A positron is just like an electron, except that it has a positive charge. However, when a proton meets an antiproton or an electron meets a positron, the particles destroy each other, disappearing in a puff of energy.

As bizarre as the concept may sound, scientists have known about antiparticles for decades.

"When I talk about antimatter to my colleagues, they

are not very excited about it. They say, 'Okay, so what's new? What are you doing with it?'" says Rolf Landua, a physicist at CERN in Geneva, Switzerland. "When I talk to nonphysicists about it, they look at me with great eyes and say, 'God, it sounds so exotic.'"

MAKING ANTIMATTER

At CERN, Landua works with a group called the ATHENA collaboration. These physicists were the first to succeed in linking positrons with antiprotons to make atoms of antihydrogen—the simplest antiatom.

In theory, the process of making antimatter is fairly simple, though the equipment needed to do it can be very complicated (and expensive).

Scientists at CERN use a one-of-its-kind machine to make antiparticles. When created, these antiparticles typically have a whole lot of energy. Inside the machine, they zoom along circular tunnels, making a million circuits every second. But on each lap, the tiny objects pass through magnetic and electric fields that slow them down. Once the antiparticles have stopped moving, the researchers can store and then combine them.

• **How do scientists make antiparticles?**

"We now have the first antiatom ever produced by humans," Landua says. "That's the new thing about our experiment."

BEGINNING OF TIME

Besides being mind-bafflingly strange, human-made bits of antimatter may provide windows into the very beginning of time.

One of the big mysteries of the universe, Landua says, is that it doesn't appear to contain any antimatter. "You probably don't spend sleepless nights wondering about why that is," he says. "But physicists do."

Here's one reason for pondering antimatter. Many physicists think that, if the universe started with a giant burst of energy called the Big Bang, it should have produced equal amounts of matter and antimatter.

But, whenever matter meets antimatter, the particles annihilate each other and disappear. So, during the very first millisecond after the Big Bang, the two types of particles should have canceled each other out.

Instead, perhaps because there was slightly more matter than antimatter in the beginning, only the antimatter disappeared, and our matter-full universe was able to form out of the leftovers. Landua and his colleagues want to find out what might have caused an imbalance.

"We study antiatoms, and we compare them with atoms to see if there are any differences—even the tiniest ones," Landua says. "This is a big question because, if there was no [imbalance] between matter and antimatter, we wouldn't exist."

SLOW GOING

Progress is slow. With current technology, ATHENA researchers can make 100 antihydrogen atoms every second. At that rate, making one gram of the stuff would take many billions of years—longer than the age of the universe itself.

It's also extremely hard to store antimatter because it gets destroyed as soon as it comes into contact with matter, which is everywhere. The researchers are trying to figure out how to make more antiatoms faster, trap them better, and hold onto them for longer periods of time.

- **Why would it take billions of years to produce one gram of anti-hydrogen with the current method?**

The possibility also remains that some chunk of anti-matter might exist elsewhere in outer space in the form of antistars or antigalaxies, Landua says. So far, searches of our universe have turned up nothing, but Landua hasn't given up hope.

"There may be other universes we cannot look into where there is a preponderance of antimatter," he says. "At least here, in our section of the universe, it doesn't seem like it. This is the mystery."

- **What happens when matter meets antimatter?**

So, being able to step into an alternative mirror universe to get away from your troubles will probably remain a long shot for a long time to come.

After Reading:

- Based on information within the article, offer a hypothesis of how the universe began. Be sure to make note of gaps, or unresolved questions, that scientists still have not been able to answer.

- Why is Rolf Landua hoping to discover antistars and antigalaxies? What possibilities might such discoveries offer scientists?

antimatter: Substance made up of antiparticles, which are subatomic particles that are equal in mass to regular subatomic particles, but have the opposite electrical and magnetic properties.

asteroid belt: A region in space between the orbits of Mars and Jupiter where most asteroids are found.

asteroids: Small, rocky celestial bodies found most often between Mars and Jupiter.

Big Bang: Massive explosion that marked the origin of the universe, which has been expanding ever since.

black holes: Celestial objects with forces of gravity so strong that everything—including light—is sucked inside them.

brown dwarf: A celestial body much smaller than a regular star that is hot enough to emit light.

comets: Celestial bodies composed mainly of ice and dust that look like round glowing heads with long tails of light.

dark energy: Space energy that exerts strong negative pressure that works to oppose the force of gravity.

dark matter: Matter that cannot be seen but that scientists believe causes many gravitational effects that can be seen.

evolution: The process of becoming more complex and organized over a long period of time.

extrasolar: Coming from or existing outside of our solar system.

galaxy: A large group of stars and other matter.

gamma rays: Photons that are given off by a radioactive substance.

gravity: The force of attraction that holds planets in their orbits around the sun and moons in their orbits around planets.

Kuiper belt: A region of the solar system that reaches from within the orbit of Neptune to 50 astronomical units past the sun (an astronomical unit, or AU, is the distance between the Earth and the sun).

mass: The amount of material an object contains.

matter: Substance that takes up space.

neutron star: A celestial body made up mainly of tightly packed neutrons that is formed when a much larger star collapses.

olivine: A greenish mineral.

Oort cloud: A round shell of comets that surrounds the sun beyond Pluto's orbit.

particle accelerators: A machine that spins electrically charged particles to very high speeds.

planetoid: A very large asteroid that is planet-like.

protons: Subatomic particles that have a positive electrical charge.

satellite: A celestial body that orbits around another, larger celestial body.

solar system: A group of planets that orbit around a central star.

spectrometer: A device that measures the size of wavelengths of light.

string theory: Scientific concept that says that the smallest particles we know of (such as electrons and quarks) are not solid masses, but can be further broken down into infinitely tiny, vibrating filaments or "strings."

supernovas: Stars that have died in a massive explosion.

wormhole: A hypothetical structure that would be a long tunnel that connects two points that are separated by time and space.

zero gravity: Weightlessness.

Books

Bond, Peter. *DK Guide to Space*. New York: DK Children, 1999.

Miller, Ron. *Extrasolar Planets*. Minneapolis: Twenty-First Century Books, 2002.

Nardo, Don. *Black Holes*. San Diego: Lucent Books, 2003.

Pasachoff, Jay M., et al. *Prentice Hall Science Explorer Astronomy*. Upper Saddle River, NJ: Prentice Hall, 2004.

Spangenburg, Ray, and Kit Moser. *The Life and Death of Stars*. New York: Franklin Watts, 2004.

Tanton, Linda Elkins. *Pluto, the Kuiper Belt, and Comets*. New York: Facts on File, 2005.

Websites

Amazing Space
http://amazing space.stsci.edu/

Caltech Geological & Planetary Sciences
http://www.gps.caltech.edu/

Hubble Space Telescope
http://hubblesite.org/

Mars Exploration Rover Mission
http://marsrovers.jpl.nasa.gov/home/index.html

Mars for Kids
http://athena.cornell.edu/kids/

The Nine Planets
http://www.nineplanets.org/

Science News for Kids
  http://www.sciencenewsforkids.org/

Spitzer Space Telescope
  http://www.spitzer.caltech.edu/

StarChild: A Learning Center for Young Astronomers
  http://starchild.gsfc.nasa.gov

page:

3: © Corel Corporation

6: X-ray; NASA/CXC/Northwestern/F. Zadeh et al.; IR;
    NASA/HST/NICMOS, Radio; NRAO/VLA/C. Lang;
    UH88/Nedachi et al.

13: NASA

17: E. L. Wright (UCLA), The COBE Project, DIRBE, NASA

20: NASA/CXC/SAO/G. Fabbiano et al.

31: NASA

34: NASA

41: NASA, ESA, and M. Brown (Caltech)

50: NASA and G. Bacon (STScl)

59: NASA, J. Bell (Cornell U.), and M. Wolff (SSI)

66: NASA

71: NASA

75: NASA/JPL-Caltech/SSC

87: Rainer Schödel (MPE) et al., NAOS-CONICA, ESO

103: NASA/ESA

EMILY SOHN is a freelance journalist, based in Minneapolis. She covers mostly science and health for national magazines, including *U.S. News & World Report*, *Health*, *Smithsonian*, and *Science News*. Emily divides her time between writing for kids and writing for adults, and assignments have sent her to countries around the world, including Cuba, Peru, and Sweden. When she's not working, Emily spends most of her time rock climbing, camping, swimming, exploring, and pursuing adventures outdoors.

TARA KOELLHOFFER earned her degree in political science and history from Rutgers University. Today, she is a freelance writer and editor with ten years of experience working on nonfiction books for young adults, covering topics that range from social studies and biography to health and science. She has edited hundreds of books and teaching materials, including a history of Italy published by Greenhaven Press. She lives in Pennsylvania with her husband, Gary, and their dog and cat.